ISBN 978-1-5283-2278-2
PIBN 10901431

English
Français
Deutsche
Italiano
Español
Português

www.forgottenbooks.com

Mythology Photography **Fiction**
Fishing Christianity **Art** Cooking
Essays Buddhism Freemasonry
Medicine **Biology** Music **Ancient
Egypt** Evolution Carpentry Physics
Dance Geology **Mathematics** Fitness
Shakespeare **Folklore** Yoga Marketing
Confidence Immortality Biographies
Poetry **Psychology** Witchcraft
Electronics Chemistry History **Law**
Accounting **Philosophy** Anthropology
Alchemy Drama Quantum Mechanics
Atheism Sexual Health **Ancient History**
Entrepreneurship Languages Sport
Paleontology Needlework Islam
Metaphysics Investment Archaeology
Parenting Statistics Criminology
Motivational

Historic, archived document

Do not assume content reflects current
scientific knowledge, policies, or practices.

POTENTIAL PRODUCTIVITY OF FOREST LANDS

IN PINE, CARLTON, AITKIN, AND SOUTHERN ST. LOUIS COUNTIES

MINNESOTA

by

Z. A. Zasada, M. L. Heinselman, and G. K. Voigt

UNITED STATES DEPARTMENT OF AGRICULTURE
FOREST SERVICE
Lake States Forest Experiment Station

In Cooperation With

OFFICE OF IRON RANGE RESOURCES AND REHABILITATION

1954

This report was prepared by the Lake States Forest Experiment Station at the request of the Office of Iron Range Resources and Rehabilitation of the State of Minnesota. In making a survey of forest resources it became apparent that the forest productivity of Pine, Aitkin, Carlton, and southern St. Louis Counties was comparatively low. This situation seemed to warrant a special analysis of the problems surrounding the productivity of forest land in the four-county area. The report which follows is in a way a local problem analysis based on assembling available information and a limited field study. Funds to finance this undertaking were furnished by the Office of Iron Range Resources and Rehabilitation and the Lake States Forest Experiment Station.

CONTENTS

U. S. Department of Agriculture, Forest Service
Lake States Forest Experiment Station 1/

Miscellaneous Report No. 30   June 1954

POTENTIAL PRODUCTIVITY OF FOREST LANDS
IN PINE, CARLTON, AITKIN, AND SOUTHERN ST LOUIS COUNTIES
MINNESOTA

by

Z. A. Zasada, 2/ M. L. Heinselman, 2/ and G. K. Voigt, 3/

INTRODUCTION

More than half of the forest area in Pine, Carlton, Aitkin, and southern St. Louis counties (fig. 1) in northern Minnesota is in poor condition. Within this region much land has been forfeited for nonpayment of taxes and present prospects for early financial returns from these lands are not encouraging. A study was made during 1953 by the Lake States Forest Experiment Station to determine the opportunities for remedying this situation. Because it was important to know the reasons for development of the present condition, the history of land use in the area was reviewed. Major problems were determined by a reconnaissance survey and limited investigations were made of some of the least understood of those observed. A few general recommendations have been made as a result of this study, for improvement in land use. Several treatments have been recommended for trial on a limited basis. The need for further research has limited the scope of the recommendations to those which offer assurance of success based on present knowledge.

1/ Maintained by the U. S. Department of Agriculture, Forest Service, in cooperation with the University of Minnesota, St. Paul 1, Minnesota.

2/ Foresters, Lake States Forest Experiment Station, Grand Rapids, Minnesota.

3/ Forest Soils Specialist, University of Wisconsin, Madison, Wisconsin.

Fig. 1. -- Area covered by this report.

BACKGROUND INFORMATION

A review of some background information on the nature and extent
of the lands involved in these four counties will help to clarify the problem. The total area of Pine, Carlton, Aitkin, and southern St. Louis
counties is 4,503,200 acres (table 1 in Appendix). Commercial forest
land occupies almost three quarters of this area. Some change in forest
area can be expected from urban and industrial expansion, and some
additional land may be cleared for agriculture, although there was little
change in area of cleared land between the 1945 and 1950 censuses. However, a major portion of these counties will remain undeveloped for industry and agriculture in the foreseeable future.

Kind and Ownership of Forest Land

The Forest Survey data indicate that the more valuable conifer
types, such as pine, spruce-fir, black spruce, and white-cedar, occupy
only 14 percent of the commercial forest area (fig. 2 and tables 2 and 3
in Appendix). An additional 17 percent is in northern hardwood, oak,
swamp hardwood, and tamarack types which at present have very limited
markets. The remaining 69 percent--over two thirds of the entire commercial forest--is occupied by brush, grass, paper birch or aspen.
Aspen is a desirable species in areas where it will produce stands of

pulpwood or timber of saw-bolt size. For various reasons, however, much of the aspen in these counties does not appear very promising in this respect. The situation with paper birch is much the same. Type deterioration has progressed furthest in Pine County where 79 percent of the commercial forest is in these less desirable types (table 4 in Appendix).

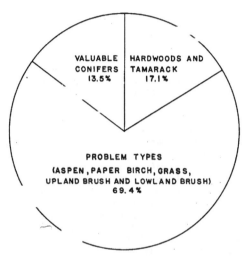

Fig. 2. -- Distribution of cover types in Pine, Carlton, Aitkin, and southern St. Louis counties, Minnesota (1948 to 1953 data).

Public agencies own 59 percent of the forest land in the problem area (fig. 3 and table 5 in Appendix). The counties alone administer almost 40 percent of the forest land (1,256,300 acres).

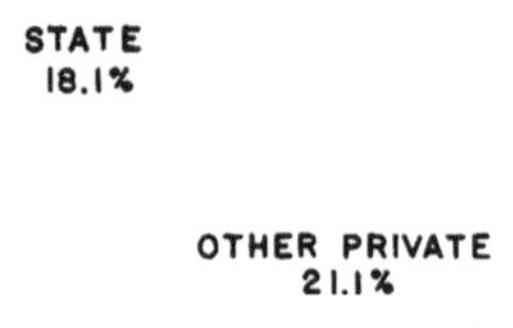

STATE   FARM
18.1%   20.2%

OTHER PRIVATE
21.1%

Fig. 3.--Ownership of commercial forest land in Pine, Carlton,
Aitkin, and southern St. Louis Counties, Minnesota
(1948 to 1953 data)

        County ownership is the result of widespread tax-forfeiture of
forest lands, on some of which taxes have not been paid since the original stand of timber was cut. Following legislation in 1935 the tax-delin-
quent lands passed to public ownership. Some land still is being forfeited each year. In recent years the counties have tried to lessen the bur-
den of carrying these lands by land sales, or through forest management.
Much of the land is unsalable at present because it is not suitable for
agriculture, or has little prospect of yielding an income from forest
crops in the near future. County stumpage sales are not possible on a
large percentage of the area because the stands are unmerchantable.
Therefore, the land probably will remain in public ownership. Its dis-
position should be determined by what the land will produce in the future. However, there is a general lack of knowledge concerning the
future possibilities of the forest lands in these four problem counties.

Soils, Climate, and History of the Area

        The present condition of forest lands in the four-county area is
the product of climate, soils, and the original forest, as modified by
man-caused factors such as logging, fire, swamp drainage, and agriculture.

- 4 -

Soils of the Area

All of the soils in the four-county area are derived from glacial deposits. The glaciation of the region involved several advances and retreats of different ice fronts, leaving a complex pattern of till plains, moraines, outwash area, and old lake beds. These glacial features are the source of most of the present topography. 4/ Certain chemical and physical properties of the soils in the area are closely correlated with the type of glacial material on which they have developed. There are three major types of drift in the four counties, each the result of a distinct ice movement (fig. 4). In central and northeastern Pine County, southern Aitkin County, eastern St. Louis County, and the scutheastern tip of Carlton County the soils have formed on "red drift" laid down by an advance of ice from the northeast. This drift is reddish in color, low in lime content, and usually sandy, gravelly, or rocky in texture, although scattered pockets of heavier soils are present. Soils formed on this drift are generally not very fertile.

4/ Information obtained from Professors H. E. Wright, Jr. and D. B. Lawrence of the University of Minnesota, and from publications by F. Leverett and F. W. Sardeson, formerly of the Minnesota Geological Survey, is the basis for the following sketch of Minnesota's glacial history.

LEGEND

GRAY DRIFT
(Gray, fine-textured, calcareous)

SUPERIOR LOBE
(Red, fine-textured, calcareous)

RED DRIFT
(Red, coarse-textured, acid)

OLDER DRIFT

DRIFTLESS AREA

SCALE - STATUTE MILES

0   15   30   45   60   75

Generalized from maps by H.E.Wright Jr., University of Minnesota, and F. Leverett and F W Sardeson, formerly of the Minnesota Geological Survey

A second and more recent advance of ice from the northwest deposited the so-called "gray drift" over northern Aitkin County, western St. Louis County, southern Pine County, and the northwestern tip of Carlton County. Soils formed from this deposit are buff-gray in color, high in lime, and usually clayey or loamy in texture, except for scattered patches of sandy outwash or gravelly moraine. Most of the area covered by this deposit is quite fertile.

The third drift resulted from an ice advance from the northeast which was contemporaneous with the ice that left the previously described "gray drift." This so-called "Superior lobe" from the northeast covered some of the older red drift with a thin deposit of reddish, high-lime material that is usually not as coarse as the older red drift. Within this region there are places where the older, low-lime red drift was not covered by this deposit, and hence forest soils may be actually formed from the latter within the limits of the Superior lobe.

In addition to these three distinct types of glacial drift there is a narrow belt of lake-laid, high-lime, red clay of the Ontonagon Association which borders the shore line of present day Lake Superior. This deposit extends only a few miles from the lake, except in the Nemadji Valley (Carlton County) where the clay runs back some 20 miles.

Scattered throughout the area are peat and muck swamps that formed in old glacial lake beds or other depressions left by the glaciers. The largest such areas in the four counties are in southwestern St. Louis County and the northern and southeastern parts of Aitkin County. The capacity of these organic soils to produce forest crops is dependent upon the depth and composition of the peat, the movement and reaction of swamp water, the character of the underlying mineral soil, and probably other factors. Relatively little is known about the reaction of swamp species to these factors.

As might be expected from the glacial history, soils in the four counties are quite varied. The combined effects of differences in texture, chemical nature, organic matter content, and topographic position make for a complex pattern of soils distribution. These differences are often of critical importance in determining which tree species will grow best in a given location. A detailed soils survey has been made of Pine County (11) but the other three counties have had only scattered reconnaissance work to date. A generalized description of the major soils associations of the four counties is available (see fig. 5).

Climate of the Four Counties

Climatic differences within the study area are due chiefly to latitude and the influence of Lake Superior. Mean annual temperatures decrease from 42°F. in southern Pine County to 37°F. at the northern border of the area. The normal frost-free season averages 130 to 140 days in southern Pine County and near Lake Superior, and only about 105 days in central St. Louis County. Mean annual precipitation varies

Fig. 5.--Major soil associations of the four counties.

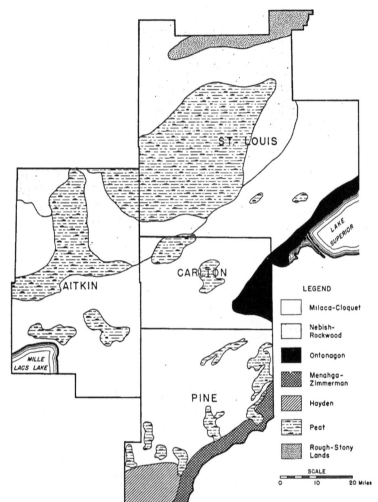

Based on "Principal Soil Regions of Minnesota" by P R McMiller, Bulletin 392
Minnesota Agricultural Experiment (Some peat areas added)

U.S.D.A. - S.C.S., Milwaukee, Wis., 1954

from 24 to 27 inches, being lightest in western St. Louis County. These differences, while superficially minor, are nevertheless sufficient to affect the natural distribution and abundance of certain tree species considerably. In southern Pine County white spruce, balsam fir, and black spruce occur very sparingly, and such hardwoods as sugar maple, basswood, yellow birch, eastern hophornbeam (ironwood), and the oaks are common. To the northeast there is a gradual increase in the abundance of the northern conifers, and a corresponding decrease in the oaks, maples, and other hardwoods. The pines, especially white pine, grow successfully throughout the area. Aspen and paper birch also are common throughout the four counties.

Original Forests

The virgin forests of the area were of a transitional nature (fig. 6). Hardwoods and mixtures of hardwoods with white pine were abundant in Pine and Aitkin Counties. Farther north, particularly in southern St. Louis County, spruce and balsam fir occurred more often, either as a spruce-balsam type or in mixtures with the pines. Forested swamps were extensive. A large percentage of Aitkin and southwestern St. Louis Counties at one time supported forests of black spruce, tamarack, and white-cedar. In Aitkin County particularly, many of these swamps are now totally deforested.

The original forests in this four-county area included about 1,000,000 acres of white and red pines, or stands in which these species were commercially prominent. It is difficult to get exact information on the quality of old-growth pine in counties such as Pine and Aitkin where most logging took place 60 to 80 years ago, but all the information available indicates that both white and red pines usually were of excellent form, size, and soundness.

Warren Upham described the forest of Aitkin County in 1896 to 1899 as follows (13):

"The species of trees most valued are the white and Norway (red) pines. These trees seldom form extensive tracts of forests, unmixed with other species, and probably no more than a quarter part of the county originally bore merchantable pine..... Where the white pine grows in abundance and of large size, it is an unfailing sign that the soil is till, but far the greater part of the till areas are mainly or solely occupied by a hardwood forest of many deciduous species, and these also often, or generally, are intermingled with white pine. Apparently the most clayey till tends to bear only hardwood, while rather gravelly and sandy till invites the growth of white pine, and extremely sandy till bears both white and red pines in varying proportions. Coming to a change of soil from the till to the modified drift, the white pines are usually found limited to the former, perhaps growing intermingled with hardwood, if the land is very clayey or with the red pine if there is less clay. On the sand and gravel areas of the modified drift, especially where they are somewhat rolling or hilly, the red pine has its best development..... The jack pine grows almost exclusively on these tracts of sand and gravel, either mixed with the red pine or alone.

"The alluvial lands bordering the Mississippi bear only very rare pines, but spruce, balsam fir and arbor vitae are occasionally found on such small portions of these lands as are swampy, and they often are plentiful, with tamarack in the frequent swamps through all the county.....

- 10 -

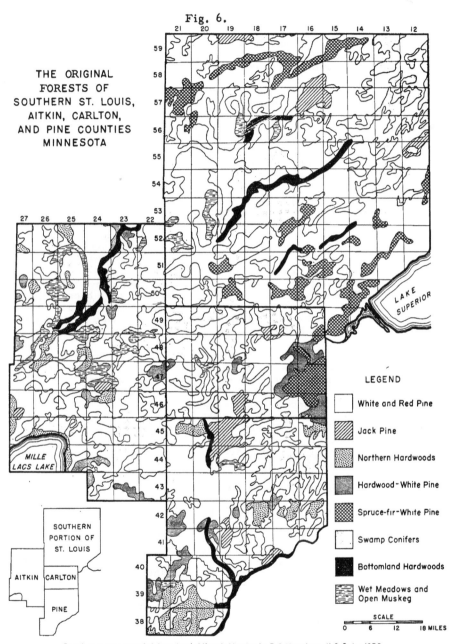

Fig. 6.

THE ORIGINAL
FORESTS OF
SOUTHERN ST. LOUIS,
AITKIN, CARLTON,
AND PINE COUNTIES
MINNESOTA

LAKE SUPERIOR

MILLE LACS LAKE

LEGEND

☐ White and Red Pine

▨ Jack Pine

▦ Northern Hardwoods

▨ Hardwood-White Pine

▨ Spruce-fir-White Pine

☐ Swamp Conifers

■ Bottomland Hardwoods

▤ Wet Meadows and Open Muskeg

SCALE
0   6   12   18 MILES

SOUTHERN
PORTION OF
ST. LOUIS

AITKIN | CARLTON

PINE

Based on a map compiled from Land Office field notes by F J Marschner, U S D A, 1930

"Hay is a natural product of the district, for portions of many of
the streams are bordered by moist lands, from a few rods to
a half mile in width, bearing a luxuriant growth of tall meadow
grasses which make one to two tons of hay per acre. All other
parts of the country are more or less wooded....."

This description of Aitkin County presents a fairly clear idea of
the extent and distribution of the various forest types in the original
forests as related to soil and drainage conditions. Since Mr. Upham
was a well known and reputable botanist as well as geologist, his descriptions are believed to be quite reliable

W. H. C. Folsom (3), writing in 1888, makes an occasional
reference to forests and other cover types as he described the early history of various Minnesota counties. In describing Aitkin County he states:
"It is a heavily timbered region, upon which the lumberman has drawn
for hundreds of millions of feet of lumber. The whole surface is dotted
with lakes and variegated with natural meadows." The latter reference
to "natural meadows" ties in with Upham's description of the meadows
bordering streams, and suggests that some of the "deforested" lowlands
in this county may never have supported timber stands within the known
past. Folsom's remarks about Pine County's forest include the following: "This county was originally heavily timbered with pine, from which
fact it derived its name. Though immense quantities have been removed,
the supply is still great enough to make the region a lumberman's par-
adise for years to come (that was in 1888). The southern townships are
heavily timbered with hardwood and are rapidly being converted into
good wheat farms."

Many other references attest to the generally valuable forest
of the present problem area. It is clear, however, that even before
logging or fires became common there were some areas of poor timber.
Apparently the very sandy outwash areas never supported more than a
fair stand of red and jack pines, and there were occasional areas of
aspen and birch. Open meadows and stagnant spruce and tamarack bogs
made up the balance of the lightly timbered or treeless area. Most of
these sparsely timbered tracts were not large enough to be mapped by
Marschner or others who mapped the original cover of the state.

History of the Forest Products Industries

Logging in the area probably began first in southern Pine county about 1838. Franklin Steele had a crew cutting pine on the Snake river, in what probably is now Pine County, in that year (2). Logging continued at an accelerated pace in the county up to the Hinckley fire of
1894. At first all of the timber was driven to the St. Croix by means of
the Snake, Kettle, and Grindstone Rivers and their tributaries. In the
1870's railroads were built from the Twin Cities to Duluth, and logs
and lumber began to move by rail as well as water. The peak of activity in Pine County was reached between 1870 and 1890, although there
were still large mills in the county as late as 1900. The Brennan Lumber Company's mill at Hinckley was cutting 200,000 board feet daily at

the time of the 1894 fire.

Aitkin County's timber was first logged in areas accessible to the
Mississippi and Rum Rivers by stream driving. The Northern Pacific
reached Aitkin in 1870-71, and railroad logging soon began to replace
river driving. Much of the early cut from this county was milled down-
stream at Minneapolis and other points along the Mississippi. By 1905
most of Aitkin County's white pine had been cut, although some industries based on hardwoods and scattered tracts of pine have persisted
down to the present day. The old "Wooden Ware Mill" at Hill City, manu-
facturing butter tubs and other hardwood products, ceased operations
in the 1920's. A large volume of cedar poles, posts, and shingles were
produced from the swamplands of the county.

Carlton and southern St. Louis Counties were cut for pine as long
ago as 1850 and 1860 in areas immediately adjacent to Duluth, but logging proceeded slowly until railroads reached Duluth in 1870. The pace
of activity then increased rapidly; Cloquet, Duluth, and Virginia became
the centers of the sawmilling industry. The St. Louis and Cloquet Rivers
and their feeders became the scene of tremendous spring drives. By
1890 the Duluth and Winnipeg Railroad had tapped the forests of the most
northern townships. The maximum cut in these counties was attained in
the decades between 1885 and 1905, the peak coming at about the turn
of the century (6).

By 1905, then, most of the big pine had been cut or burned in the
four counties, except for scattered tracts that were less accessible or
poorer in quality. As the cut of pine declined rapidly a new type of forest industry gradually began to develop. Pulp and paper mills were
constructed at Cloquet, Brainerd, and Grand Rapids, and a new type of
sawmilling operation based on small portable mills appeared. Markets
now began to open up for black spruce, balsam fir, and later on even
the "weed trees," aspen and jack pine. A match and toothpick factory
at Cloquet, and veneer mills in Wisconsin supplied an outlet for birch
and the better northern hardwoods. Poles, piling, and mine products
continued to be cut on a smaller scale.

These new industries provided a continuing market for the scattered parcels of pine and better hardwoods that remained. Most of the
uplands in the region were completely cutover and burned-over by 1920,
leaving such isolated tracts as the only source of raw materials for the
new industries. The result was a further "culling" of the forest area,
as one by one these last remnants of better quality timber were cut.

Then came the thirties and a further decline in the forest industries. In the meantime, however, "second growth" of aspen, birch and
jack pine began to develop, and pulpwood volumes in these species began to swell. Unfortunately, in the counties being studied the area of
good quality second growth was not large. Those stands that were operable found a ready market during the recent war years. Cutting in the

past 15 years, then, has of necessity been confined to the better stands, since little else was salable at all. This situation has led to a further deterioration of the area's forests.

History of Forest Fires in the Area

Forest fires have played a major role in shaping the second-growth forests of the four-county area. Following is a brief outline of fire history in the area.

The great Hinckley fire of September 1, 1894, and the Cloquet, Moose Lake, and other fires of the 1918 disaster are still recalled vividly by some residents. These fires took a tremendous toll of human lives, property, and timber, and created heat so intense that in some places the organic layer of the soil was almost entirely consumed. The fires of these two seasons left their mark on the four counties' forest resource by wiping out the last sources of conifer seed over large areas, and consuming or severely damaging reproduction and young growth on hundreds of thousands of acres.

But devastating as these fires were, the second-growth forests of today might have looked far more promising on much of the area had these been the only fires. The less spectacular ones that took no human lives, but killed or severely set back the struggling young stands each spring and fall for perhaps 30 to 60 years, are a factor that must be carefully considered if the present forest situation in these counties is to be understood.

"Burning over" lands that were to be cleared for agriculture was a common practice of local settlers until about 1918 or 1920, and even more recently in some townships. Logging companies normally disposed of their slash by broadcast burning from about 1907 to 1920 as a means of "hazard reduction" to protect settlements. In the decade 1916 to 1926, 27 percent of all fires were caused by land clearing, 22 percent by railroads, and 21 percent by smokers and campers; miscellaneous causes including logging accounted for the other 30 percent (7).

The problem counties have had the unenviable reputation of having one of the poorest fire records in the state since fire statistics first were maintained. Certain townships in each county have had from 35 to over 100 reported fires in the past 10 years, according to records of the State Division of Forestry. This situation is reflected in the slow recovery of the second-growth forests of the area.

The History of Swamp Drainage

In the early days of land settlement in this area even responsible government officials, soils men, and engineers were optimistic about the agricultural possibilities of the region's swamplands. Many of these swamps supported good stands of tamarack, spruce, and white-cedar, but little thought was given to growing forest crops as a permanent use for such lands. Most of the stands were logged off or burned off with the thought that the swamp would soon be put to agricultural use. It was generally believed that drainage was all that would be needed to make these areas productive.

Beginning about 1905, an extensive system of ditches was installed in the larger swamp areas, and the settlers began to move in. Ditching was generally financed by county ditch bonds. Ditches were usually spaced at mile intervals along section lines, although closer or wider spacings were sometimes used. It was soon found that drainage was inadequate, clearing was costly, and markets poor. The few settlers that attempted to farm these lands were forced to abandon their enterprise, except on an occasional well located tract where the peat was very shallow and the drainage good.

Most of the drained swamps were never cultivated, but the ditches exposed dried peat surfaces to fire, and the burning of peat lands became an annual occurrence. Vast swamps became totally deforested and full of burned-out pockets where the peat had been consumed to depths of several feet. Many of these swamps which once supported good forests are now producing nothing but sedges, cattails, and wild marsh grasses. Small acreages are cut for marsh hay in dry years, but most of this wild forage is of poor quality and is not utilized. Much of the forested swampland remaining is badly understocked as a result of clear-cutting and fire, and there are now some 611,900 acres on which lowland brush is virtually the only woody vegetation left. The majority of these deforested swamps are now in public ownership through tax-forfeiture.

THE PRESENT PROBLEM

Out of the historical background just reviewed has come the present problem with which this report is concerned. Fires, unrestricted logging, unwise drainage of swamps, and misdirected agriculture have left these four counties with approximately 1,800,000 acres of potential forest land that is now producing little or no income except for what game, berries, and wild hay may be harvested. The remaining 1,300,-000 acres of the commercial forest area is in better condition, but could be producing much greater yields of timber if stocking and species composition were improved. The problem is one which should concern all the people of Minnesota because of the poor condition of these strategically located forest lands.

Answers to the following questions will aid in determining whether investments should be made by the public to rehabilitate these lands.

1. What are the primary causes of the poor condition of the forest in these counties?

2. How much of the land now stocked with aspen and birch is suited to the permanent management of these species? Will other species produce merchantable forests on lands not suited to aspen and birch?

3. Will the present understocked areas of aspen saplings produce merchantable yields of timber? If not, is there a practicable method for improving these stands?

4. To what extent can natural processes be expected to restore conifers or other valuable species on lands now supporting only poor aspen, birch, or brush?

5. Are there economic methods of planting, seeding, and plantation care for restoring valuable forest growth to the poorly stocked upland and deforested swamp areas?

HOW THE STUDY WAS MADE

This analysis of the current forest situation was made from data compiled from published reports and records dealing with the area, and from data collected in an extensive examination of timber and soil conditions. The reports consulted were state fire records, old books and pamphlets, soil survey reports, economic reports, and Forest Survey reports which dealt with the land problem of northern Minnesota.

The field work dealt primarily with soil and timber stand conditions. Particular attention was paid to the aspen type which is the largest single forest type and which occurs on a variety of soil conditions.

Soils samples and descriptions and complete stand and site data were collected on the best and poorest aspen sites that could be located. The red drift soils of northeastern Pine County were sampled extensively since they were considered representative of the poorer aspen lands. Gray drift soils were checked in southwestern St. Louis County and in adjacent counties in connection with an over-all study of aspen sites. Upland brush areas were checked to determine whether the soils where brush is a problem differed significantly from those of aspen lands.

RESULTS OF THE STUDY

The Effects of Forest Fires

The history of forest fires has already been reviewed briefly.

However, to fully appraise the effects of fire a more detailed study is necessary.

Because it was impractical to cover the whole area, Pine County was selected for a detailed analysis of the actual fire history to determine to what extent fire is responsible for the present condition of the county's forest resource. Maps showing all reported fires in the county for the period 1923 to 1951 (fig. 7), supplied by the State Division of Forestry, were studied to obtain as clear a picture as possible of the distribution and frequency of reported fires.

The fires were segregated into three occurrence groups to show the extent of repeat burning in given areas. It became apparent that some townships, such as T. 42 N., R. 18 W., and T. 42 N., R. 17 W., have been burned over almost completely in the past 30 years, and many areas within these townships were burned over two or more times in that period. Tax-forfeiture is high in nearly all of the heavily burned townships.

The fire record for all reported fires in the state for the years 1915 to 1924 (fig. 8) shows that many of the same areas in Pine County that burned over since 1923 also were burned during the previous decade. From 1915 to 1924 the other problem counties had a fire record similar to that for Pine County. During this period fires in Pine County were more concentrated in the northwest portions of the county; since 1923 they have been more prevalent on the east side.

Fire records are scanty prior to 1915, but a rough approximation can be made of the areas burned in the Hinckley disaster of 1894, and a more detailed map is available of the 1918 fires (fig. 9). Comparison of records (figs. 7, 8, and 9) show that many areas in Pine County that have had no reported fires since 1923 were burned over by the Hinckley (1894) or Bruno (1918) fires, or by other fires from 1915 to 1924. In the absence of actual fire records the areas burned over prior to 1915 must remain a matter of conjecture except for the rather sketchy map of the Hinckley fire. However, there is good reason to believe that earlier unrecorded fires covered much of Pine County. Logging camps, settlers, and railroads were present in various parts of the county from about 1870 up to 1915, the first year for which fire occurrence records are readily available. This is a period of 45 years in which fire protection was in its infancy, yet logging debris was abundant, and there was little regard for fire prevention. It is generally believed that forest fires burned more area in these early years than in recent decades. If this is true, then there can be little doubt that most of Pine County has been burned over from one to three or more times in the past 80 years. A parallel history is believed to exist for Aitkin, Carlton, and southern St. Louis Counties, but time would not permit detailed verification.

Another line of evidence which emphasizes the role that fires have played in these counties can be found by tracing the origin of present

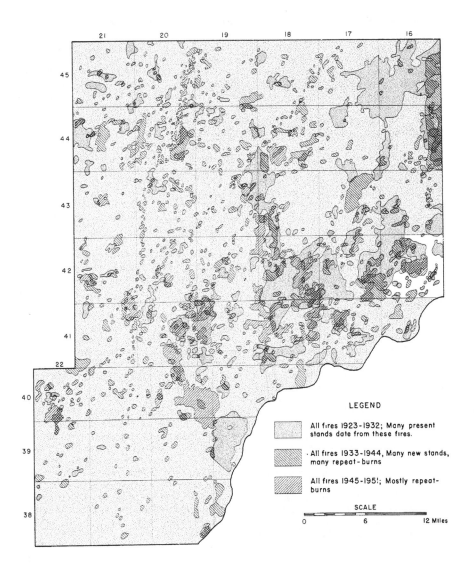

LEGEND

All fires 1923-1932; Many present
stands date from these fires.

All fires 1933-1944, Many new stands,
many repeat-burns

All fires 1945-1951; Mostly repeat-
burns

SCALE

0   6   12 Miles

Fig. 7.--Reported forest fires in Pine County, Minnesota, 1923-1951.

Based on Fire Occurence maps of the Minnesota Division of Forestry

U S.D-A. - S C S , Milwaukee, Wis., 1954

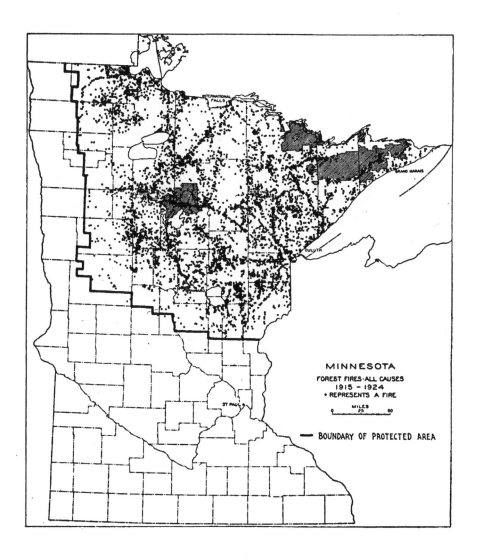

MINNESOTA

FOREST FIRES-ALL CAUSES
1915 - 1924
• REPRESENTS A FIRE

MILES
0   25   50

— BOUNDARY OF PROTECTED AREA

Fig. 8 --Location of forest fires, all causes, Minnesota, 1915 - 1924.
(Reproduction of fig. 19, p. 35, "Forest Fires in Minnesota,"
by J. A. Mitchell.)

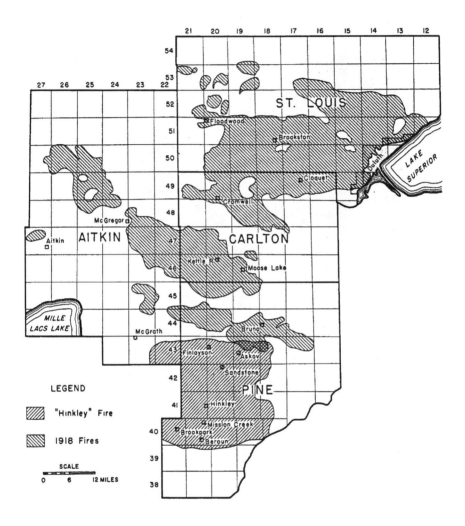

Fig. 9.--Approximate areas in problem counties burned by the
"Hinckley" (1894) and 1918 fires.

timber stands. Many areas that are known to have been logged 40 to 70 years or more ago now support scrub "second growth" only 10 to 35 years old. Scattered trees of older age classes are sometimes found in such stands, and when they are, they often bear the scars of one or more fires. Where evidence such as this is found, it is safe to assume that there have been repeat burns that killed most of the previous stand and started a new crop of aspen suckers, or birch or hardwood sprouts. Further proof that this has occurred on large areas in these counties can be obtained by analyzing sample tree records of the recent Forest Survey (table 1).

It is a striking fact that 80 percent of the aspen type in Pine County is less than 30 years old, much of it only 10 to 20 years old. Had there been no repeat burning in Pine County, one would expect the present aspen stands to date from the original slash fires which in most cases burned soon after logging was completed. Since the original logging of this county took place largely between 1870 and 1900, most of the aspen type should be between 53 and 83 years of age now. Obviously, then, there was widespread destruction of these first aspen stands, presumably by fire, since comparatively little of the second-growth aspen has been logged. The presence of large areas of 10- to 30-year-old aspen indicates that in much of Pine County the most recent fires that were severe enough to wipe out the previous stands occurred within the last three decades.

Many young stands of aspen and birch have been burned through by light surface fires that were not severe enough to kill a major portion of the trees. This fire damage usually can be detected by basal scars on remaining trees, and by a generally understocked and ragged appearance of the stand. A large percentage of the fires in Pine County since 1933 (fig. 7) caused this type of damage. A parallel situation is believed to exist in the other three counties. The total area of aspen damaged by such creeping surface fires probably runs into the hundreds of thousands of acres for the area as a whole.

Now, just what has this fire history meant in terms of present forest conditions? For the upland areas it has meant conversion from what might have been valuable second-growth forests to vast acreages of brush, grass, and injured, understocked stands of aspen, paper birch, and sprout hardwoods. These species have taken over because they are the most successful in withstanding the effects of repeated fires. Aspen maintains itself through its ability to produce root suckers, while birch, the oaks, basswood, and some other hardwoods resprout from fire-killed stumps. Conifers on the other hand reproduce primarily from seeding; once destroyed, artificial seeding or planting is necessary.

Table 1.--Area of the aspen type in Pine County - by size and age class

(1953 data)

Size class	Average age class (years)						Total
	0 - 10	11 - 20	21 - 30	31 - 40	41 - 50	51+	
	Acres	Acres	Acres	Acres	Acres	Acres	Acres
Saw timber	0	0	0	300	1,300	1,000	2,600
Pole timber	0	0	17,400	29,600	10,300	7,100	64,400
Restocking	45,500	58,400	12,800	0	0	0	116,700
Understocked	11,700	42,700	4,000	0	0	0	58,400
Total	57,200	101,100	34,200	29,900	11,600	8,100	242,100

A study of the effect of fire on the growth of quaking aspen (12) led to these conclusions:

"It appears that the fire history of the stand is one of the most important factors affecting aspen site quality. In the past this fact has generally been overlooked, especially as regards the effect of repeated burning. In pine or other conifer stands, basal scars and 'catfaces' leave an obvious record of burning for decades after the occurrence of the fire. In aspen it is not particularly obvious 10 to 20 years after burning, due to more rapid rotting and disappearance of the badly damaged trees, and because of the rapid healing over and apparent recovery of those less severely burned. Fire is a great aid to the establishment of the aspen type on lands formerly occupied by conifers or northern hardwoods, but burning after aspen is established has serious consequences. It reduces growth, causes fire scars that open the way for decay, reduces stocking and volume, and causes site retrogression, early senility and breakup of the stand. Fires consume all or parts of the litter, F and H layers, thus destroying much of the vast network of fine feeding rootlets in the lower portions of the organic layer. The burning of the organic layers reduces the amount of nitrogen for plant growth and decreases infiltration and water holding capacity. Fires also open the stand to invasion by competing weeds and grasses; the latter appear to prevent optimum stand development."

To sum up, then, repeated fires have deteriorated the quality of second-growth forests in the four counties in the following ways:

1. Species composition has been adversely affected by the removal of valuable conifers and some hardwoods, and by their replacement with the less valuable aspen, paper birch, and sprout hardwoods.

2. Stocking has been seriously reduced by the death of many firekilled or injured trees; understocking is so serious that many stands of mature or nearly mature timber do not contain enough volume to make commercial logging operations feasible.

3. Growth rates have been drastically cut down in stands that have survived repeat-burns.

4. Injury of trees that survived forest fires has left wounds that serve as a means of entry for disease and insect attack - factors that are often responsible for the early decadence and breakup of stands that might otherwise have lived to a greater age and larger size.

5. Over half a million acres of swampland have been totally deforested by a combination of drainage and fire.

- 23 -

6.   An additional 369,400 acres of upland have been taken over by a cover of grass and brush due to repeated fires and grazing.

Soil-Site Factors

Aspen, which comprises the largest cover type in the area, occurs on all upland soils in the four counties studied. Some of these soils lack the soil moisture and other properties that are associated with good aspen growth and development. Coarse-textured soils which have a deep ground water table and are deficient in organic matter usually are poor aspen sites. Generally these soils also possess a relatively low pH value and a low content of available nutrients. Soil analyses of samples taken from sample plots show that soils with these general characteristics are widely distributed in the four counties. Examples of soils of this type are the Omega, Onamia, and Emmert sands. Excessive drainage may also occur in soils of medium texture underlain by coarse gravelly material. Much of the Cloquet fine sandy loam exemplifies these conditions. This soil type is quite extensive in the four-county area.

Productive aspen sites usually exhibit soils properties which are correlated with favorable soil moisture conditions. These include a moderately high content of soil organic matter, a fairly high content of silt and clay-sized particles, a moderate to high content of nutrient elements and in many cases close proximity of the ground water table. Soils with these characteristics cover a substantial acreage of the study area and are generally more abundant in the gray drift region. Most of the upland soils in the four-county region range between these two extremes. Past experiences have shown that the soils in this intermediate group are capable of producing commercial yields of aspen trees.

The physical properties of upland soils are modified to a great degree by the type and amount of organic matter present in the upper part of the soil profile. This is especially true of the water-holding capacity andthe rate of infiltration of water into the soil. In addition, the organic fraction of upland soils serves as a storehouse of essential nutrient elements such as nitrogen, phosphorus, potassium, calcium, and magnesium. For these reasons the role of organic matter attains its greatest importance in light-textured, excessively drained soils with an inherent low level of fertility. Removal of the organic layer by fire disrupts the moisture and nutrient regime and considerably lowers or reduces the site quality for aspen growth. This effect, which is most critical on the coarser textured soils, has occurred in varying degrees over most of the four-county area.

In addition to poor quality aspen, a large acreage of coarse-textured soils in the four-county area bear pine, paper birch, grass, upland brush, or oak. These soils are best suited to the growth of jack and red pines. The medium- and fine-textured soils which have been severely depleted by fire also are better adapted to the growth of species such as red pine and white spruce. The large acreage classified as lowland brush occurs on peat and muck. Swamp conifers were the original forest cover on these soils. Reforestation of these sites is handicapped by lack of knowledge of site classification and planting methods for swamps.

To some extent observations of natural plant communities are useful for evaluating the role which soil and other factors play in determining site quality, although this relationship may be somewhat obscured where fire has almost totally destroyed the original vegetation, as in much of this area.

Early work on this subject at the Lake States Forest Experiment Station indicated approximately the following sequence of aspen site and natural plant communities (5, 8):

Natural plant community	Site quality for aspen
Ash - elm	Good
Northern hardwoods	Good
Spruce - balsam fir	Medium
Oak	Medium
White pine	Medium
Jack pine - red pine	Poor
White-cedar	Poor
Tamarack - black spruce	Very poor

Classification of the present aspen-birch type in the four counties according to its original cover indicates the following acreage of aspen sites:

Original cover	Estimated acreage of present aspen type	Site quality
Ash - elm	31,000	Good
Northern hardwoods	100,000	Good
Spruce - balsam fir	487,000	Medium
White pine	343,000	Medium
Jack pine - red pine	85,000	Poor
Swamp conifers	46,000	Poor

Assuming that the plant indicator approach is valid for areas as heavily burned as these counties, there should be 131,000 acres of aspen type on lands that are capable of growing high-quality aspen products, 830,000 acres on land that should at least grow pulpwood and sawbolts, and 131,000 acres on sites that are better suited for other species.

The Effects of Climate

The effects of climate on the growth of the important timber species in the area have never been systemically investigated. It is worth noting that most of the species common to this region approach either the southern or northern limits of their natural ranges within the four counties. In Minnesota, aspen, paper birch, the spruces, balsam fir, and red pine are all near their southern limit in Pine County. For red pine this may mean little, since its natural range lies in a comparatively narrow band across the northeastern states and climatic conditions in the four counties are probably close to the optimum for this species. Quaking aspen, black and white spruces, and balsam fir belong to the boreal forest and their optimum range is farther north.

For this reason, it is possible that the yield and quality of aspen products may not be as high in the southern portion of the counties studied as those which are obtained in the species optimum range. The same principle applies to sugar maple, yellow birch, and most of the oaks which approach their northwestern limit in northern Minnesota.

Disease and Insect Factors

Tree diseases and insects have played a role in shaping the current forest situation. Disease and insect pests of aspen are the most important. Recent investigations of Hypoxylon canker (1), a serious cause of mortality in aspen, have indicated that the incidence of this disease is distinctly higher in the southern portion of Minnesota's aspen forest than in the more northern counties. The area in question is thus in a region where heavy Hypoxylon losses can be expected.

The recent study showed that incidence of Hypoxylon is not correlated with any of the site factors investigated, but that damage is more serious on poor sites, apparently because the slower growing trees are exposed to infection longer before reaching merchantable size. A strong tendency for this disease to be more common in understocked stands also was found. For the four-county area these facts probably mean that losses from Hypoxylon will be an important cause of reduced yields from aspen stands for some time to come.

Heart rots, top rots, and root rots also are important causes of increased cull and mortality in aspen, hardwoods, and balsam fir in the four counties. Insects, particularly the poplar borer, birch borer, forest tent caterpillar, larch sawfly, and carpenter ants frequently cause losses in growth and contribute to mortality. Wounds caused by ground fires have probably served as a means of entry for insects and diseases on a large scale in the study area.

Natural Replacement of Poor Aspen with Better Species

Ecologists and foresters have pointed out that the aspen normally is a temporary type. There is evidence to show that in the absence of forest fires or logging, nature would replace the aspen forest with stands of balsam fir, spruce, sugar maple, basswood, oak, and in some cases pine. The question of immediate concern is how soon will conversion of aspen to more valuable species take place in the four-county area.

Pine trees of seed-producing size are lacking over much of the aspen type in this area. Studies made by the Lake States Forest Experiment Station show that to be effective seed trees must be both plentiful and well distributed. Studies have shown that in most of the aspen area pine establishment has been retarded by an inadequate seed supply, poor seedbed conditions, excessive plant competition, and feeding by deer and hare. Therefore, it can be concluded that the natural return of pine on these aspen lands will not occur for many decades to come.

Balsam fir is much better adapted than pine to growing under aspen, and it is gaining a foothold on a considerable area of aspen land in St. Louis and northern Aitkin and Carlton Counties. Where balsam fir is coming in, the eventual replacement of aspen by this species can be encouraged by fire protection and care in logging. Since balsam fir is a good pulping species, this type change is probably desirable. Balsam is less common in the southern portions of the area, and cannot be counted on to replace aspen on a large scale there.

Sugar maple, basswood, and the oaks are coming in farther south wherever a seed source remains. The quality of these new hardwood forests, however, may not be much better than that of the aspen which they are replacing.

A study of the extent of natural conversion in Minnesota (4), using data from the current Forest Survey, has indicated the approximate percentage of aspen type in the four counties that may be replaced by other types (table 2).

These type changes may occur within the next 10 to 60 years, depending upon the age of the present aspen stand and its understory of hardwoods, balsam fir, spruce, or pine. These figures, of course, are only a forecast of what could happen if fires and logging do not interfere with natural trends. In practice, some of the understories will be lost through logging damage or fire, hence the total of conversions through natural processes may not be as large as indicated.

This work only serves to emphasize the gradual, long-term aspects of "letting Nature do it." It is true that Nature, if left alone, eventually would mend the damage done by past misuse, but the question is, can we afford to wait that long? Natural conversion, then, may be a partial answer on perhaps 380,000 acres within 60 years, but what of the other 712,000 acres?

Almost half of the aspen type may develop sufficient volume to permit cutting. Much of this area will then become a permanent aspen type to be managed for aspen production. The remaining half million acres either is growing on soils not suited to the production of aspen, or has been so ravaged by fire that there is little likelihood of the present stands ever reaching merchantability. Natural conversion to better species is believed to be proceeding very slowly on this acreage. On this

Table 2.--Area of aspen in the four counties that may naturally convert to other cover types within the next sixty years (1951)

(Acres)

Type aspen is converting to	Area by counties				Total
	Pine	Carlton	Aitkin	Southern St. Louis	
Spruce - fir	1,500	19,700	12,900	69,600	103,700
Swamp conifer	0	1,500	6,600	5,200	13,300
Pine	7,200	3,500	6,600	12,500	29,800
Oak	21,800	0	0	0	21,800
Ash - elm	17,400	9,200	6,400	32,700	65,700
Northern hardwoods	30,500	11,200	22,800	39,500	104,000
Mixed types	13,100	4,100	9,900	14,600	41,700
Little or no conversion	150,600	97,500	118,600	345,500	712,200
Present total aspen area	242,100	146,700	183,800	519,600	1,092,200

area a rehabilitation program of some sort will be necessary if forest crops are to be harvested within the foreseeable future. If nothing but fire protection is supplied on the poorer areas it is difficult to say just what would replace the present aspen. Probably a scattered growth of oak, maple, basswood, and a few conifers, with occasional aspen and paper birch of various ages would result. Brush also would remain a problem for a long time.

Possible Improvement Through Fire Protection

A large share of the denuded land and poor-quality aspen can be laid to the repeated fires in the four-county area. Will protection from fire, then, reverse the trend of deterioration? There are numerous stands of medium or better stocking where protection may bring through a merchantable crop of pulpwood. Protection from fire will stop the depletion of soil organic matter under such stands and prevent further losses in stocking and vigor through the injuries inflicted by surface fires. Where a minimum of 5 to 10 cords per acre of salable wood can be expected, an eventual harvest will pave the way for a second crop of better quality. Cutting of the old stand will create conditions of light and soil temperature suitable for aspen suckering, and a new stand can be counted on to develop if a reasonably clean clear cut of the former stand is obtained. If protected from fire, this new generation of aspen suckers should be much better in quality than its predecessor for the following reasons:

a. Fire protection will result in a build-up of soil organic matter and improvement in physical properties of the soil.

b. The new sucker stand should be fully stocked and without the injury of fire this stocking will be maintained, giving higher volumes per acre, and less exposure to disease, insect, and windstorm damage.

c. Without the injurious effects of surface fires growth rates should be better, and the stands should maintain their vigor to a greater age and larger size.

Many sites that are barely producing a merchantable yield in the present rotation may therefore produce 10 to 20 or more cords per acre of good quality pulpwood in the second rotation.

Fire protection will permit an expansion of the present area in conifers. The present stands of pine, balsam fir, and spruce will gradually seed adjacent areas. If these stands remain unburned, these types will in time expand in acreage. However, to encourage this expansion, the seed source must be maintained by wise cutting practices applied in the remaining stands.

The denuded and more seriously understocked areas will not be helped materially by fire protection alone. On a large portion of this area, however, tree growth and forest conditions gradually will become established. However, there definitely are large areas where fire protection alone will not solve the problem within 20 to 40 years.

MEASURES FOR FOREST IMPROVEMENT

This review of the forest situation shows that fire has created most of the poor forest conditions. It is essential, therefore, that land burning be kept to a minimum if forest conditions are to improve. If the local people will support and cooperate with the protection organization of the Minnesota Division of Forestry, the fire problem can be solved here as it has been in other areas.

Management of the Higher Value Forest Types

Within the four counties there are 47,100 acres in pine, 174,400 acres in upland spruce-balsam fir, and 306,300 acres of swamp conifers. An additional 226,000 acres are growing northern hardwoods and oaks, some of which are of commercial quality. A large percentage of these better types are understocked or are too young to be merchantable. The operable area in high-value types, therefore, is very small at present. It is imperative that these areas be protected from fire and managed under good forest practices so that further depletion of better species will not occur. If logging operations are conducted according to the best silvicultural recommendations available, the present area in valuable types can be maintained and will also provide some cutting. These scattered blocks of good timber will then serve as a seed source which will gradually expand the acreage of pine, spruce, balsam fir, swamp conifers, and the better hardwoods.

Aspen Land Management

Following fire the problem of greatest concern is how to handle the aspen type. It is known that aspen does grow well and can be a profitable crop on much of the area it occupies. Lands on which aspen is established that are not suited to its growth should be converted to more suitable species. Accordingly, aspen stands should be classified as to their adaptability to the sites they occupy. A general aspen classification survey, although desirable, may be impractical or impossible for lack of funds. However, before any work such as logging, clearing, or planting is undertaken, the land should be classified as to its potential for producing aspen, since this factor can have an important bearing on the economic and silvicultural success of the forest improvement operation. During the early life of a pure aspen stand it is often difficult, even for a professional forester, to determine the adaptability of aspen for quality production. In the four-county area studied, fire disturbance has

- 30 -

further complicated site conditions. However, guides have been devel-oped which permit a fairly reliable site classification. The procedure, as brought out in the discussion on soils, is quite lengthy since it requires a knowledge of the original stand, a soil classification, and information on water table. Further research work on aspen sites is being done and is necessary if aspen management is to be improved and a simplified procedure is to be found for identifying good aspen producing areas.

Survey estimates indicate there are about 490,000 acres of aspen type on lands capable of producing good aspen yields. Less than half of this area is well stocked and only about 20 percent supports a merchantable crop. However, aspen should be continued as a crop on this land for at least another rotation. The following management methods are recommended for this acreage.

1.   Well stocked stands which now have commercial yields, or are capable of producing merchantable yields, should be harvested at rotation age. Harvest age will vary with stand conditions and past stand history; it may be as low as 35 years. Good quality stands should be grown until 50 or 55 years old. At harvest there should be a complete clear cut of the aspen. Good trees of desirable species such as pines, oaks, spruces, and balsam fir should be reserved to encourage a mixed forest. Well stocked young stands on favorably situated good sites may lend themselves to intensive management. Here, through non-commercial thinnings and partial cuts, a more valuable crop of aspen can be raised on a short rotation.

2.   Partially stocked stands made up of trees not suited for logging present a second condition class present on good aspen sites. These stands either can be converted to other species or put back into aspen production. In view of the large area needing planting it is recommended that these areas be reproduced to aspen. Very little work has been done on similar lands to restore aspen. However, there are two approaches that merit trial. One is to make a complete clear cut of the stand. In this event some usable wood can be produced to help defray the cost of the project. A second method is disking. Since these methods are not proven, "pilot plant" trials are suggested. Such trials could be undertaken by the Office of Iron Range Resources and Rehabilitation with technical assistance from research agencies.

3.   Good aspen sites which have not reproduced well and have only scattered stocking could be disked to increase the aspen stocking. Such trials have proved successful in Wisconsin, Upper Michigan, and Minnesota. The cost of this work has been as low as $2.50 per acre.

The area of "off-site" aspen and heavily burned land not suited to aspen production is estimated at 602,200 acres. Some of this area will produce a small harvest of pulpwood. The objective for these lands should be ultimate conversion to species suited to the site. Tests carried out by the Lake States Forest Experiment Station in northern Minnesota have brought out the essential requirements for successful conversion practice. Briefly these requirements are: (1) The soil must be prepared thoroughly in advance of planting. (2) The overstory should be thinned enough to allow 50 percent light to penetrate it. (3) Only thrifty, high-quality planting stock with a minimum height of 6 inches should be used. Classes of stock recommended are jack pine 1-1, red pine 2-1, 1-2, or 2-2, white spruce 2-2 or 2-3, balsam fir 2-2 or 2-3. The choice of species should be governed by the soil. (4) Trees should be planted closely, about 4 x 6 feet. (5) Annual releases should be provided for until the trees are free from competing underbrush. (6) After trees are 4 to 5 feet high the overstory should be completely removed. Present methods for conversion are expensive and will run a minimum of $50.00 per acre (10).

In undertaking a conversion planting program the following planting site preference is recommended: (1) Areas severely burned and supporting only scattered aspen. These areas can be reforested at the lowest cost. (2) Second priority should be aspen areas with stands less than 12 feet in height. Experience in conversion planting has been that costs increase sharply as the stands get larger. (3) Poor site areas with merchantable stands should be planted immediately following logging.

A large-scale project of converting aspen lands to other species is not recommended at this time because of lack of experience in methods, cost, and success of such undertakings. A small-scale conversion project should be tried to gain experience in this work. This project could be in the form of establishing a scattering of block plantings 10 to 40 acres in size throughout the four-county area. In time these plantings could form a seed source for natural conversion.

Further research is recommended on methods of conversion. Trials in the use of herbicides would be desirable as a method of controlling the aspen. Use of portable chippers to permit the harvest of wood on off-site areas should be tried (studies show that wood from poor sites is equal in quality to that from good sites). Following harvesting, spraying with herbicides to control suckering, and machine planting may be feasible.

Deforested Swamps

There are 611,900 acres of lowland brush, now deforested, which formerly supported a commercial stand of swamp conifers. To date little experience has been gained in restoring conifers on swamplands. Large-scale work on these lands should be deferred until results have been obtained on experimental areas.

Studies carried out by the Lake States Forest Experiment Station indicate that seeding of black spruce, and planting of black spruce and tamarack can be successful under certain conditions. The procedures developed in these plot studies should be expanded on a pilot-plant basis.

Reforestation of Upland Non-restocking Areas

An estimated 369,400 acres of upland in the study area now support only brush and grass. The primary consideration on these areas is whether their highest use may be forest production, game production, and, in a few instances, agriculture.

Unlike deforested swamps, methods have been developed for reforestation of grassy and brushy uplands and old fields (9). Except for open sandy fields some form of ground preparation is necessary to insure successful plantation establishment on these lands. Plantation care should be recognized and provided for in reforestation programs. Planting programs that continue without providing for plantation care usually build up a future obligation which is difficult to meet and can result in plantation losses. Advice on planting methods, equipment use, and stock requirements should be sought from forest agencies that have had considerable experience with tree planting.

Planting costs vary as to planting chance. Present planting costs of brush lands, including stock, field planting, and overhead costs, will run $30.00 to $35.00 per acre. Open areas planted by machine with no advance ground preparation will cost somewhat less.

Early returns can be obtained from well stocked plantations. Thinnings can be made for Christmas trees, posts, pulpwood, and small poles. In Wisconsin and Michigan, returns which exceeded the cost of planting were received from thinnings for Christmas trees as early as 10 years after planting. Several plantations in Minnesota are providing similar returns.

SUMMARY OF PROGRAM NEEDED

The forest improvement measures discussed indicate the need for a large-scale program requiring a considerable expenditure of funds to restore the forest lands of the four-county area to full productivity. Work should not be deferred, because the area has many advantages from the viewpoint of forestry investment and intensive management. The area is strategically located in relation to markets and large centers of population. The wood-using centers of Cloquet and Duluth are within the study area. Minneapolis, St. Paul, the farming area of Minnesota, and the wood industries of Wisconsin, are within favorable shipping distances for forest products.

The accessibility of the area is better than average for the forest area of Minnesota. There are several railroad lines serving the area. The network of state, county, and township roads makes most of the area accessible for year-round logging.

Therefore, even though resources may limit the scope of an improvement program, the following summary of suggested measures should offer ample opportunity for productive use of funds available:

1. Insure effective protection from fire through support of Minnesota Division of Forestry.

2. Stimulate good management of areas of quality types currently merchantable.

3. On good aspen sites:
    a. Harvest well-stocked stands at rotation age by making a complete clear cutting of the aspen, but saving good trees of pines, spruces, balsam fir, and oaks.
    b. Apply intensive management measures to well-stocked young stands on good sites.
    c. Make "pilot-plant" trials of the present recommended methods for getting poorly stocked stands on good aspen sites into full production.

4. Initiate a program of getting "off-site" aspen lands and heavily burned lands converted to species suited to the site.

5. Expand the research work in methods of restoring conifers to swampland.

6. Determine the highest use for the abandoned fields and upland brush areas. Those areas suited to forest should be restored to production by planting.

LITERATURE CITED

(1)   Anderson, Ralph L.
        1952   Factors influencing the incidence of Hypoxylon canker
                of aspen. (Unpublished Ph.D. thesis, Univ. of Minn.)

(2)   Burnquist, J.A.A.
        1924   Minnesota and its people. Vol. 1, 572 pp. Chicago,
                Clarke Publ. Co.

(3)   Folsom, W.H.C.
        1888   Fifty years in the Northwest. 763 pp. St. Paul,
                Pioneer Press.

(4)   Heinselman, Miron L.
        1951   The extent of natural conversion to other species in
                the Lake States aspen-birch type. (Unpublished Mas-
                ter's thesis, Univ. of Minn.)

(5)   Kittredge, Joseph, Jr.
        1938   The interrelations of habitat, growth rate, and asso-
                ciated vegetation in the aspen community of Minnesota
                and Wisconsin. Ecol. Monog. 8: 153-246.

(6)   Larson, Agnes M.
        1949   History of the white pine industry in Minnesota.
                Minneapolis, Univ. of Minn. Press, 432 pp., illus.

(7)   Mitchell, J.A.
        1927   Forest fires in Minnesota. Minn. Forest Service,
                74 pp., illus.

(8)   Roe, Eugene I.
        1935   Forest soils - the basis of forest management. Lake
                States Forest Experiment Station, 9 pp., illus.
                (Processed.)

(9)   Rudolf, Paul O.
        1950   Forest plantations in the Lake States. U. S. Dept.
                Agr. Tech. Bul. 1010, 171 pp., illus.

(10)   Shirley, Hardy L.
        1941   Restoring conifers to aspen lands in the Lake States.
                U. S. Dept. Agr. Tech. Bul. 763, 36 pp., illus.

(11)   Simmons, C. S., et al
        1941   Soil survey of Pine County, Minnesota. U.S. Dept Agr.,
                Bureau of Plant Industry in coop. with Univ. of Minn.
                Agr. Exp. Sta., Series 1935, No. 15, 44 pp., illus.

(12) Stoeckeler, Joseph H.
        1948   The growth of quaking aspen as affected by soil
                properties and fire. Jour. Forestry 46: 727-737.

(13) Winchell, N. H., et al
        1899   The geology of Minnesota. Geol. and Nat. Hist.
                Survey of Minn., Vol. 4. St. Paul, Pioneer Press Co.
                629 pp., illus.

APPENDIX

Table 1 - Area of land by use and by counties (1948-1953 data) [1]

Status class	Pine Acres	Carlton Acres	Aitkin Acres	Southern St. Louis Acres	Total Acres	Percent
Commercial forest land	526,500	369,400	893,900	1,391,700	3,181,500	70.6
Non-commercial forest land	32,400	21,100	48,200	104,600	206,300	4.6
Cropland and cleared pasture	242,300	81,000	139,700	170,200	633,200	14.1
Urban, industrial, roads and other non-forest	102,500	78,900	85,600	215,200	482,200	10.7
Total area in county	903,700	550,400	1,167,400	1,881,700	4,503,200	100.0

[1] Based on County Forest Resource Surveys conducted by the Office of Iron Range Resources and Rehabilitation, and the Lake States Forest Experiment Station, 1948-1953.

Table 2 - Commercial forest areas by cover types and counties (1948-1953) [1/]

Cover type	Pine Acres	Carlton Acres	Aitkin Acres	Southern St. Louis Acres	Total Acres	Commercial forest area Percent
White pine	200	4,300	2,600	5,000	12,100	0.4
Red pine	400	1,300	2,600	4,300	8,600	.3
Jack pine	7,400	3,200	2,000	13,800	26,400	.8
Spruce-fir	7,700	14,900	13,600	138,200	174,400	5.5
Spruce	8,100	16,200	40,100	106,200	170,600	5.4
Tamarack	5,300	3,500	39,400	52,800	101,000	3.2
Cedar	0	1,300	17,300	16,100	34,700	1.1
Northern hardwoods	40,200	20,600	101,900	39,200	201,900	6.3
Oak	16,300	3,700	4,100	0	24,100	.8
Bottomland hardwoods	23,000	21,200	106,900	66,500	217,600	6.8
Aspen	242,100	146,700	183,800	519,600	1,092,200	34.3
Paper birch	24,600	7,500	23,900	80,600	136,600	4.3
Grass-upland brush	47,900	61,800	183,400	76,300	369,400	11.6
Lowland brush	103,300	63,200	172,300	273,100	611,900	19.2
All types	526,500	369,400	893,900	1,391,700	3,181,500	100.0

1/ Based on County Forest Resource Surveys conducted by the Office of Iron Range Resources and Rehabilitation, and the Lake States Forest Experiment Station, 1948-1953.

Table 3 - Commercial forest areas by counties and size classes (All types combined)(1948-1953) 1/

Size class	Pine Acres	Carlton Acres	Aitkin Acres	Southern St. Louis Acres	Total Acres	Commercial forest area Percent
Saw timber	21,600	13,300	42,200	22,200	99,300	3.1
Pole timber	107,700	73,000	226,300	324,600	731,600	23.0
Restocking	156,600	127,300	165,100	587,400	1,036,400	32.6
Understocked	240,600	155,800	460,300	457,500	1,314,200	41.3
Total	526,500	369,400	893,900	1,391,700	3,181,500	100.0

1/ Based on County Forest Resource Surveys conducted by the Office of Iron Range Resources and Rehabilitation and the Lake States Forest Experiment Station, 1948-1953.

Table 4 - Area of "problem types" by counties (1948-1953) [1]

Cover type	Pine	Carlton	Aitkin	Southern St. Louis	Total	Commercial forest
	Acres	Acres	Acres	Acres	Acres	Percent
Aspen	242,100	146,700	183,800	519,600	1,092,200	34.3
Paper birch	24,600	7,500	23,900	80,600	136,600	4.3
Grass-upland brush	47,900	61,800	183,400	76,300	369,400	11.6
Lowland brush	103,300	63,200	172,300	273,100	611,900	19.2
Total	417,900	279,200	563,400	949,600	2,210,100	69.4
Percent commercial forest	79.4	75.6	63.0	68.2		

1/ Based on County Forest Resource Surveys conducted by the Office of Iron Range Resources and Rehabilitation, and the Lake States Forest Experiment Station, 1948-1953.

Table 5 - Ownership of commercial forest land in Pine, Carlton, Aitkin, and Southern St. Louis Counties, Minnesota (1948-1953)[1]

Class of ownership	Pine Acres	Carlton Acres	Aitkin Acres	Southern St. Louis Acres	Total Acres	Total Percent
County and municipal (mostly tax-forfeited)	207,600	132,800	275,100	640,800	1,256,300	39.5
State (includes Aitkin County ditch lien lands)	71,600	38,900	346,100	120,500	577,100	18.1
Federal (includes Indian Trust)	1,200	13,000	6,900	13,200	34,300	1.1
Farm	147,100	143,400	157,600	193,400	641,500	20.2
Other private	99,000	41,300	108,200	423,800	672,300	21.1
Total (commercial)	526,500	369,400	893,900	1,391,700	3,181,500	100.0

[1] Based on County Forest Resource Surveys conducted by the Office of Iron Range Resources and Rehabilitation, and the Lake States Forest Experiment Station, 1948-1953.

Nature of Soils in Study Area

In the field soils were studied by (1) excavating trenches sufficiently to expose the complete soil profiles, (2) describing the soil profiles, and (3) collecting soil samples from the various horizons for laboratory analysis. Field tests were made for soil reaction and soil texture.

After collection the soil samples were air-dried, passed through a 20-mesh sieve, and analyzed by the following methods: reaction-electrometrically using a glass electrode; content of sand, silt, and clay by a hydrometer method; exchange capacity by leaching with N ammonium acetate and subsequent distillation and titration; conductance by determining the resistance of a 1:2.5 suspension of soil in water; content of available calcium, magnesium and potassium by leaching with N ammonium acetate and determining the content of cations in the leachate by means of a Beckman spectrophotometer; content of available phosphorus by a stannous chloridemolybdate method; content of organic matter by titration; total nitrogen by the Kjeldahl method.

A brief description of the forest stand, characteristic ground cover vegetation, and the soil profile for each plot follows:

Plot 1. Pine County (Sec. 27, T. 43 N., R. 18 W.):

Forest cover: primarily aspen; 65 feet at 50 years; yield -12 cords; understory of red maple.

Ground cover: meadow rue, large leaf aster, bracken fern, strawberry and Rubus spp.

Soil: melanized gley loam (Freer series).

A_0	2-0 inches	Matted, partly decomposed leaf litter and organic remains.
A_1	0-3 inches	Dark brown to dark gray fine sandy loam containing earthworms.
A_2	3-9 inches	Grayish brown to brown sandy clay loam.
B	9-20 inches	Slightly structured brown silty clay loam with some mottling in the lower portion.
G	20 inches	Gray sandy clay loam with greenish and reddish mottling. Free of roots. Ground water evident at 36 inches.

Stones and small boulders scattered throughout the profile.

Plot 2.   Pine County (Sec. 9, T. 43 N., R. 18 W.):

> Forest cover: medium to poor aspen; 51 feet at 35 years; yield 12 cords; diseased trees abundant; former white pine site; understory of hazel, swamp fly-honeysuckle and mountain maple.
>
> Ground cover: bunchberry, strawberry, blackberry, bracken fern, false Solomon's seal and grasses and sedges.
>
> Soil: melanized gley loam (Freer series).

A_0	2-0 inches	Matted, partly decomposed litter held together by roots of ground cover vegetation.
A_1	0-4 inches	Dark brown very fine sandy loam to silt loam. The upper half inch of this horizon consists of charcoal.
A_2	4-6 inches	Slightly lighter grayish silt loam. Not sharply defined and may be absent. This horizon may be masked by organic matter from decomposing grass roots.
BC	6-30 inches	Mixed red and gray sandy loam. Red color and clay content increase with depth.
G	30 inches	Reddish gray mottled sandy clay. Ground water at 55 inches.

Large stones scattered in upper 24 inches of the profile. Some shale present. Stratified layers of sand, gravel, and clay occur at 6 feet.

Plot 3.   Pine County (Sec. 27, T. 42 N., R. 18 W.):

> Forest cover: medium to poor aspen; 56 feet at 36 years; poorly stocked; many diseased trees; dense understory of hazel and alder with some dogwood.
>
> Ground cover: bunchberry very abundant; large leaf aster, Rubus spp., meadow rue, club moss, and grasses and sedges.
>
> Soil: melanized sand (Cloquet series).

A_0 2-0 inches   Matted, partly decomposed organic remains held together by roots of ground cover vegetation.

A_1 0-5 inches   Dark brown medium sand. The upper half inch of this horizon consists of charcoal.

A_2 5-10 inches   Light brown sand. This horizon is not well pronounced and in some cases may be entirely absent.

B 10-20 inches   Brown to reddish brown sand. Slightly compacted.

C_1 20-36 inches   Reddish brown sand mottled with grayish brown sand.

C_2 36 inches   Dark reddish brown compacted moist sand. No evidence of ground water at a depth of 5 feet. In some cases one inch of gray clay occurs at 4 feet.

Plot 4.   Pine County (Sec. 17, T. 42 N., R. 18 W.):

Forest cover: fair to good aspen; 70 feet at 50 years; yield 20 cords per acre. Some elm and black ash with an understory of hazel, alder and swamp fly-honeysuckle.

Ground cover: bunchberry, meadow rue, anemone, bracken fern, Rubus spp., Hypnum moss, and grasses and sedges.

Soil: podzolized gley loam (Adolph series).

A_0 3-0 inches   Matted, well decomposed organic remains of forest and ground cover vegetation.

A_1 0-1 inch   Dark brown to black silt loam. Absent in some profiles. No evidence of charcoal.

A_2 1-6 inches   Light gray clay loam.

B 6-20 inches   Reddish brown structured clay.

C 20 inches   Reddish clay becomes mottled with bluish gray clay at a depth of 30 inches. No root penetration beyond this depth. In some cases this mottled clay is underlain by very fine sand. Ground water evident at 50 inches.

Plot 5.   Pine County (St. Croix Park, Sec 10, T. 40 N., R. 18 W.):

Forest cover: poor aspen; 47 feet at 54 years; yield 8 cords per acre; some white spruce, balsam fir, and red maple; jack pine, red pine, white pine, bur oak, and red oak occur on surrounding ridge.

Ground cover: wintergreen, pyrola, starflower, aster, blueberry, blackberry, raspberry, grasses and sedges and reproduction of white pine and balsam fir.

Soil: podzolic sand (Omega series).

A_0 2-0 inches   Matted, partly decomposed litter and ground cover remains. Fungus mycelia are abundant.

A_1 0-1 inch   Brown medium sand stained with organic matter.

A_2 1-8 inches   Grey medium sand.

B   8-20 inches   Reddish brown medium sand. Very slightly cemented.

C   20 inches   Coarse red sand. Slight mottling at 7 feet.

Plot 16,   Carlton County (Cloquet Experimental Forest, Sec. 31, T. 49 N., R. 17 W.):

Forest cover: medium to poor aspen; 49 feet at 50 years; yield - 16 cords per acre. Some large-toothed aspen occurs scattered throughout the area. This area was cut for red pine around 1905 and has not been burned since that time.

Ground cover: wintergreen, aster, bracken fern, blueberry and grasses and sedges.

Soil: podzolic sand (Omega series).

A_0 2-0 inches   Matted dark brown layer of litter and organic remains.

A_1 0-1 inch   Dark gray sand. A loose mixture of humus and sand.

A_2 1-3 inches   Grayish brown medium sand.

B   3-20 inches   Grayish brown to yellowish red medium sand. Very slightly cemented.

C 23 inches   Yellowish red water-laid sand which becomes coarser with increasing depth.

Table 6 - Reaction, texture, content of organic matter and exchange capacity of soils of different aspen sites of northeastern Minnesota

PLOT NO. 1

Horizon and depth (Inches)	Reaction pH	Sand (2.0-0.02 mm) Percent	Silt (0.02-0.002mm) Percent	Clay (0.002mm) Percent	Organic matter Percent	Exchange capacity Mil.-egs. per 100 g.
A_0 2-0	5.5				80.1	52.6
A_1 0-3	5.9	70.4	16.0	13.6	2.8	16.9
A_2 3-9	5.8	68.3	20.4	11.3	0.3	6.7
B^2 9-20	6.0	56.4	26.2	17.4	0.5	10.2
G 20	6.7	54.6	23.9	21.5	0.6	12.1

PLOT NO. 2

Horizon and depth (Inches)	Reaction pH	Sand (2.0-0.02 mm) Percent	Silt (0.02-0.002mm) Percent	Clay (0.002mm) Percent	Organic matter Percent	Exchange capacity Mil.-egs. per 100 g.
A_0 2-0	5.5				80.0	50.1
A_1 0-4	5.6	69.3	16.2	14.5	1.7	17.8
A_2 4-6	5.5	74.9	12.8	12.3	0.5	9.1
B 6-15	5.9	59.1	27.8	13.1	0.9	14.9
C 15-30	6.0	54.2	35.7	10.1	0.3	11.1
G 30	6.5	53.6	32.3	14.1	0.4	13.6

Table 6 - Reaction, texture, content of organic matter and exchange capacity of

soils of different aspen sites of northeastern Minnesota-- Continued

PLOT NO. 3

Horizon and depth (Inches)	Reaction pH	Sand (2.0-0.02 mm) Percent	Silt (0.02-0.002 mm) Percent	Clay (0.002 mm) Percent	Organic matter Percent	Exchange capacity Mil.-egs. per 100 g.
A0 2-0	5.7				87.3	46.2
A1 0-5	5.5	84.2	13.8	2.0	2.1	10.3
A2 5-10	5.0	83.1	14.8	2.1	0.3	5.8
B 10-20	5.2	80.3	13.7	6.0	0.4	6.7
C 20-36	6.3	87.2	.9.9	2.9	0.1	5.1

PLOT NO. 4

Horizon and depth (Inches)	Reaction pH	Sand (2.0-0.02 mm) Percent	Silt (0.02-0.002 mm) Percent	Clay (0.002 mm) Percent	Organic matter Percent	Exchange capacity Mil.-egs. per 100 g.
A0 3-0	5.9				76.1	58.9
A1 0-1	5.7	65.0	24.5	10.5	2.3	21.1
A2 1-6	5.2	60.4	24.3	15.3	0.8	12.7
B 6-20	6.0	20.4	33.9	45.7	0.9	17.3
G 20	6.8	8.2	42.1	49.7	0.4	17.8

Table 6 - Reaction, texture, content of organic matter and exchange capacity of soils of different aspen sites of northeastern Minnesota--Continued

PLOT NO. 5

Horizon and depth (Inches)	Reaction pH	Sand (2.0-0.02 mm) Percent	Silt (0.02-0.002 mm) Percent	Clay (0.002 mm) Percent	Organic matter Percent	Exchange capacity Mil.-egs. per 100 g.
A0 2-0	5.0				91.7	30.9
A1 0-1	5.0	80.7	17.2	2.1	1.7	10.1
A2 1-8	5.0	81.2	16.8	2.0	0.3	3.9
B 8-20	5.3	87.1	6.6	6.3	0.5	2.8
C 20-36	6.0	89.5	6.9	3.6	0.1	2.7

PLOT NO. 16

Horizon and depth (Inches)	Reaction pH	Sand (2.0-0.02 mm) Percent	Silt (0.02-0.002 mm) Percent	Clay (0.002 mm) Percent	Organic matter Percent	Exchange capacity Mil.-egs. per 100 g.
A0 2-0	4.8				72.0	62.7
A2 0-3	4.5	64.3	26.1	9.6	0.4	6.9
B 3-20	5.6	72.2	20.2	7.6	0.2	5.2
C 20-35	6.0	88.3	8.1	3.6	0.1	3.9

Table 7 - Conductance and content of essential nutrients in soils
of different aspen sites of northeastern Minnesota

PLOT NO. 1

Horizon and depth (Inches)	Conductance mhos x 105	Total nitrogen Percent	Available potassium Parts per million	Available phosphorus Parts per million	Available calcium Parts per million	Available magnesium Parts per million
A0 2-0	35.0	0.49	352	32	3870	540
A1 0-3	8.5	0.13	120	21	2100	215
A2 3-9	4.1	0.03	11	10	220	104
B 9-20	4.3	0.04	44	13	990	270
G 20	6.8	0.04	65	10	1540	295

PLOT NO. 2

A0 2-0	30.5	0.42	375	27	3600	495
A1 0-4	3.9	0.09	110	18	1210	305
A2 4-6	3.0	0.06	52	10	995	230
B 6-15	5.0	0.07	60	18	1170	385
C 15-30	6.0	0.02	60	12	1050	390
G 30	7.8	0.04	72	16	1425	486

Table 7 - Conductance and content of essential nutrients in soils

of different aspen sites of northeastern Minnesota--Continued

PLOT NO. 3

Horizon and depth (Inches)	Conductance mhos x 10^5	Total nitrogen Percent	Available potassium Parts per million	Available phosphorus Parts per million	Available calcium Parts per million	Available magnesium Parts per million
A_0 2-0	37.1	0.37	220	26	980	210
A_1 0-5	9.8	0.08	93	16	450	155
A_2 5-10	3.9	0.02	37	6	230	42
B 10-20	4.7	0.03	52	8	365	61
C 20-36	4.3	0.02	70	7	495	90

PLOT NO. 4

Horizon and depth (Inches)	Conductance mhos x 10^5	Total nitrogen Percent	Available potassium Parts per million	Available phosphorus Parts per million	Available calcium Parts per million	Available magnesium Parts per million
A_0 3-0	45.5	0.61	298	38	4320	580
A_1 0-1	8.0	0.11	139	20	1395	300
A_2 1-6	4.3	0.06	110	9	715	165
B 6-20	5.0	0.06	254	8	1980	535
G 20	6.7	0.04	110	11	2430	620

Table 7 – Conductance and content of essential nutrients in soils
of different aspen sites of northeastern Minnesota--Continued

PLOT NO. 5

Horizon and depth (Inches)	Conductance mhos x 10⁵	Total nitrogen Percent	Available potassium Parts per million	Available phosphorus Parts per million	Available calcium Parts per million	Available magnesium Parts per million
A0 2-0	18.6	0.28	220	20	956	180
A1 0-1	5.6	0.08	77	12	389	75
A2 1-8	2.3	0.02	45	7	110	40
B 8-20	2.0	0.02	59	10	190	50
C 20-36	1.5	0.01	45	7	350	78

PLOT NO. 16

A0 2-0	32.0	1.29	330	25	984	210
A2 0-3	6.2	0.05	77	5	115	23
B 3-20	4.9	0.03	150	10	352	60
C 20-35	3.5	0.02	10	7	390	65

The results of the soils analyses presented in tables 6 and 7, show that the plots with the highest yields of aspen are characterized by soils with a relatively high content of silt and clay particles, a high base exchange capacity, a high specific conductance, a high content of total nitrogen and a high content of available nutrients.

CPSIA information can be obtained
at www.ICGtesting.com
Printed in the USA
BVHW07s1308280918
528774BV00021B/1359/P